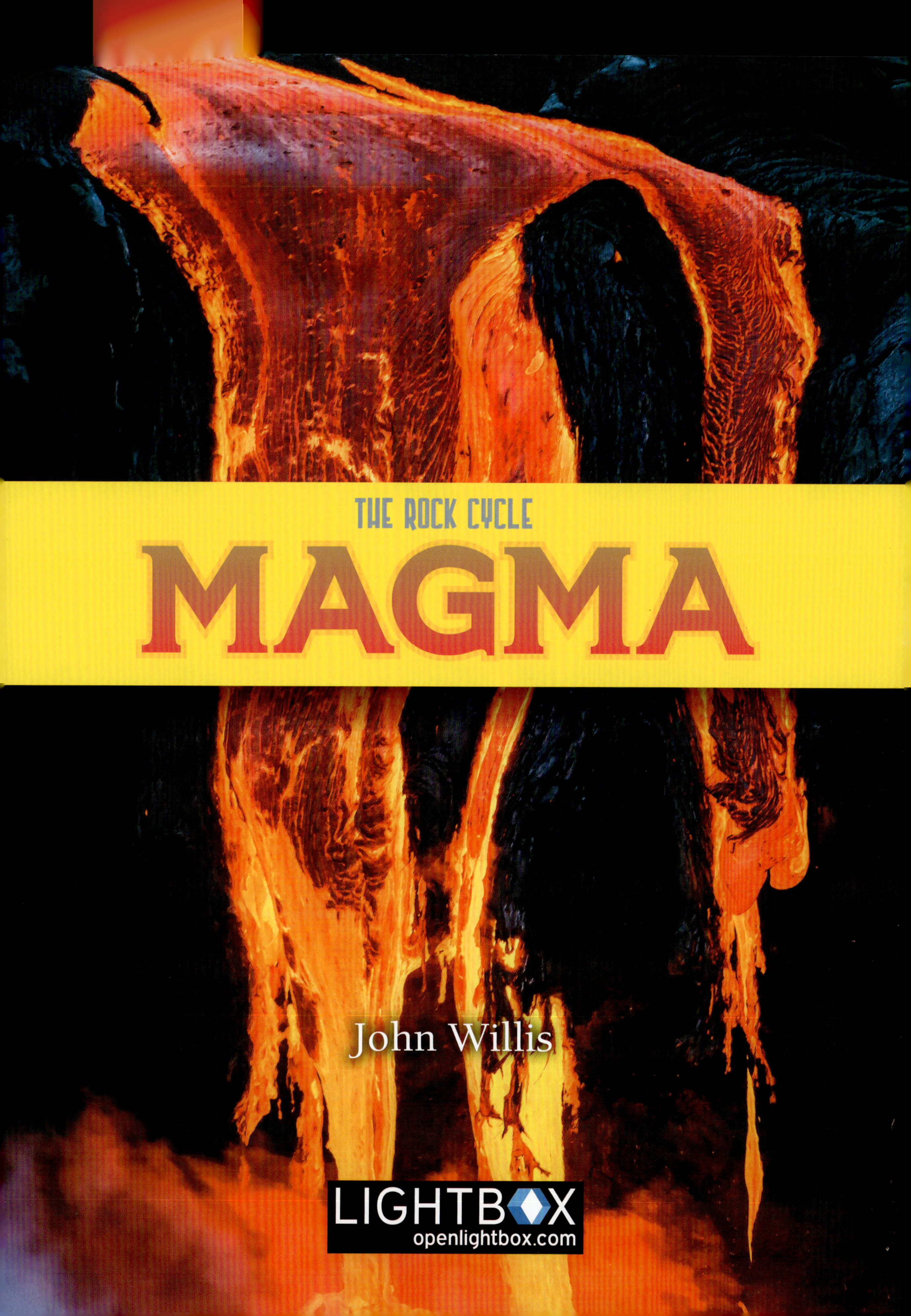

THE ROCK CYCLE

MAGMA

John Willis

LIGHTBOX
openlightbox.com

Go to
www.openlightbox.com
and enter this book's
unique code.

ACCESS CODE

LBXY6336

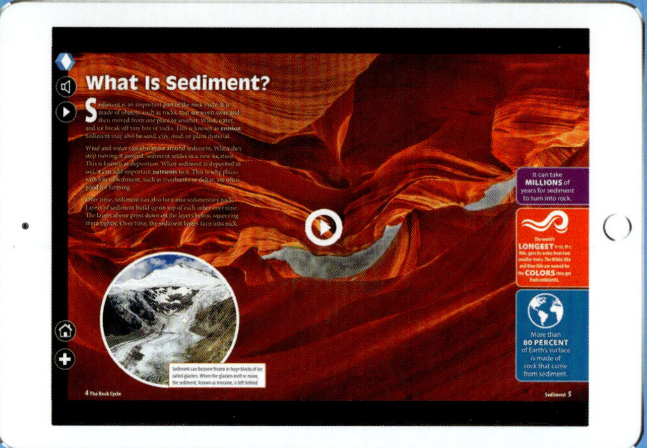

Lightbox is an all-inclusive digital solution for the teaching and learning of curriculum topics in an original, groundbreaking way. Lightbox is based on National Curriculum Standards.

STANDARD FEATURES OF LIGHTBOX

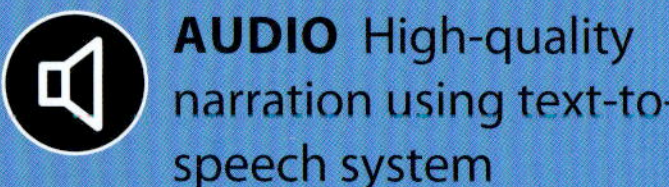
AUDIO High-quality narration using text-to-speech system

ACTIVITIES Printable PDFs that can be emailed and graded

SLIDESHOWS Pictorial overviews of key concepts

VIDEOS Embedded high-definition video clips

WEBLINKS Curated links to external, child-safe resources

TRANSPARENCIES Step-by-step layering of maps, diagrams, charts, and timelines

INTERACTIVE MAPS Interactive maps and aerial satellite imagery

QUIZZES Ten multiple choice questions that are automatically graded and emailed for teacher assessment

KEY WORDS Matching key concepts to their definitions

Contents

What Is Magma?

Earth is made of several layers. The outer layer, called the **crust**, is solid. Beneath the crust is the **mantle**. It is made of solid rock and liquid magma. Magma is hot, melted rock. Most magma is found deep inside the ground.

Sometimes, magma can reach Earth's surface by moving through holes or cracks in the crust. Magma that reaches Earth's surface is known as lava. When lava cools, it becomes a solid.

Magma is an important part of the **rock cycle**. It helps **recycle** one kind of rock into another. It can create new land, such as islands, when it cools.

Magma and lava hold small amounts of gases, including sulfur and carbon dioxide. These can be dangerous when released.

Magma can turn into **MORE THAN 700** different kinds of rocks.
The mantle is about **18.6 MILES** (30 kilometers) **BELOW** Earth's **SURFACE**.
The word **"LAVA"** was first used in **1737**.

Types of Magma and Lava

There are three types of magma. Each type is made of different **minerals** and exists at different temperatures. Basaltic magma is the hottest. It is hotter than 1,742 degrees Fahrenheit (950 degrees Celsius). Basaltic magma is high in the minerals iron and magnesium, which affects the types of rocks it can become.

Rhyolitic magma is the rarest and coldest type of magma. It is between 1,202 and 1,382 degrees Fahrenheit (650 and 750°C). Unlike basaltic magma, rhyolitic magma is low in iron and magnesium. However, it is high in potassium and sodium. The third kind of magma is andesitic magma. Andesitic magma has some of the same minerals found in basaltic and rhyolitic magmas in balanced amounts. Its temperature is between 1,382 and 1,742 degrees Fahrenheit (750 and 950°C).

Most lava comes from basaltic magma. Like magma, lava is sorted into different types. These types have different appearances and flow over Earth's surface in different ways.

PAHOEHOE

- a Hawai'ian word describing lava with a smooth, shiny surface
- made of liquid rock with a thin crust on the outside that looks like wrinkled rope
- flows by extending "toes" of lava

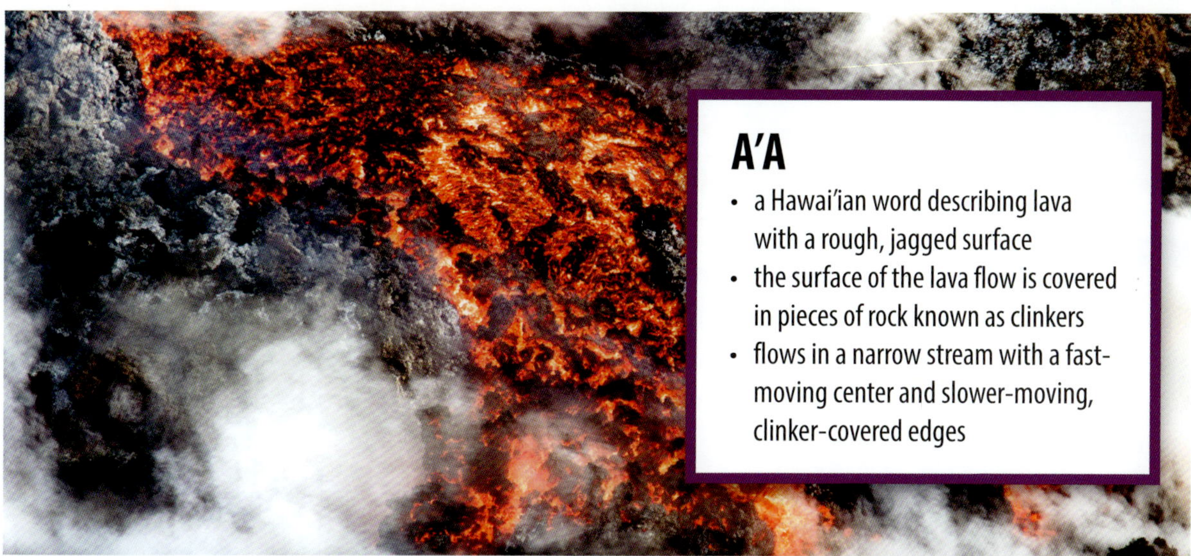

A'A

- a Hawai'ian word describing lava with a rough, jagged surface
- the surface of the lava flow is covered in pieces of rock known as clinkers
- flows in a narrow stream with a fast-moving center and slower-moving, clinker-covered edges

PILLOW LAVA

- created when magma reaches Earth's surface underwater
- the water begins to cool the outside of the lava, creating a more solid outer layer with hot, liquid lava inside
- ancient pillow lava can be used by scientists to help tell if an area was once underwater

BLOCK LAVA

- formed from andesitic or rhyolitic magma
- similar to a'a lava, but with smoother pieces of rock along its surface
- grows higher as it flows

Magma and the Rock Cycle

The rock cycle is a slow process that recycles rocks. The material that makes up rocks is not destroyed. Instead, rocks change from one type to another. The rocks have changed, but the materials they are made from have not. The rock cycle moves very slowly. It can take millions of years for one bit of rock to move all the way through the rock cycle. As part of the cycle, rocks break down into **sediments** over time. The rocks on Earth today are made from the same material as the rocks that were on Earth when dinosaurs lived.

Magma both creates new rocks and breaks down old rocks as part of the rock cycle. Earth's mantle is much hotter than its surface. This heat causes rocks to melt and turn into magma. Some magma reaches Earth's surface through **volcanoes**. There, it cools and creates new igneous rocks. Over many years, these new rocks will go through the same cycle. Some will turn into different types of rocks and then melt back into magma.

The process in which magma or lava turns into rock is known as solidification.

HOW THE ROCK CYCLE WORKS

Over time, all types of rocks break apart and become sediments. **Weathering** and **erosion** causes sediments to gather and pile up. Pressure pushes the sediments together. This creates sedimentary rock.

High temperature and pressure cause rock to melt. When melted rock cools, it forms igneous rock. Heat and pressure also change sedimentary and igneous rocks into new rocks, called metamorphic rocks. Over time, these new rocks break down into sediment once again.

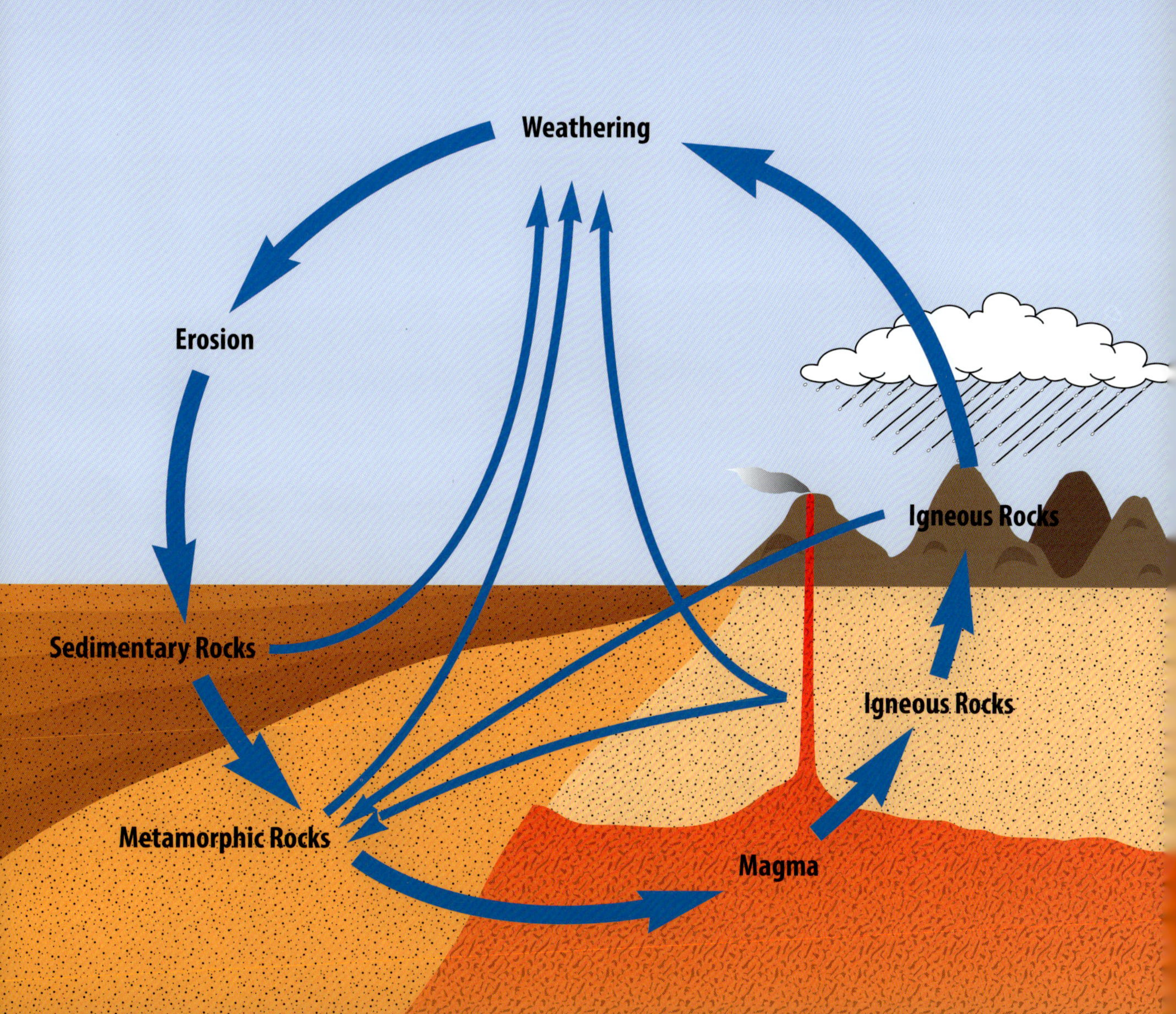

Forming Rocks

Igneous rocks are the oldest and strongest kinds of rocks. There are two types of igneous rocks. These are extrusive and intrusive. The type of igneous rock formed depends on where magma or lava cools and how long it takes to cool.

Extrusive rocks form when a volcano **erupts**. Lava pours out of the volcano. The lava may cover the land or flow into the sea. The air or water cools the lava until it hardens into rock. This can form large areas of solid rock. When a volcano erupts with a great deal of force, gases in the rocks expand very quickly. This makes holes, or pores, in the rocks.

The Giant's Causeway in Northern Ireland is made of igneous rock. It formed over millions of years as lava hit the ocean and cooled.

Intrusive rocks form when magma is pushed between layers of other kinds of rock in Earth's crust. This magma hardens more slowly than on the surface. It may form **sills** as it cools in flat underground areas. It can also form columns and chunks, called batholiths. Intrusive rocks can sometimes be found on Earth's surface. This happens when the rocks above them are worn away by weather or other forces.

Many igneous rocks have crystals. They form when magma or lava cools. This process is called crystallization. Large crystals form slowly over millions of years. They are created as rocks cool slowly underground. These crystals can be about 1 inch (2.5 cm) in size. Small crystals form when rocks cool quickly, giving the crystals less time to grow. These crystals may be too small to see. Some igneous rocks, such as obsidian, have a glassy texture. They have very few or even no crystals at all.

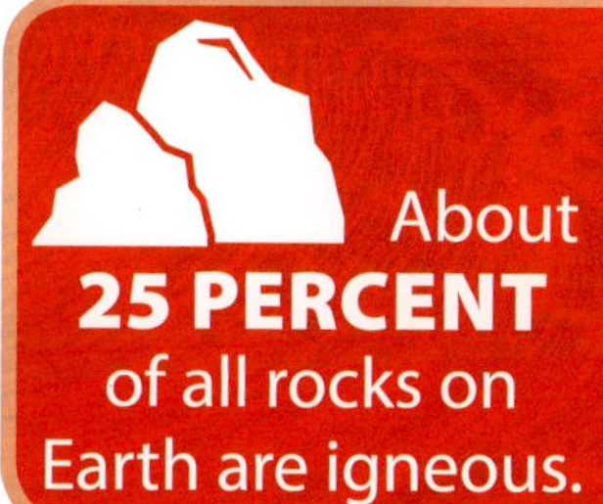

About **25 PERCENT** of all rocks on Earth are igneous.

About **65 PERCENT** of Earth's outer layer is made up of **IGNEOUS ROCK**.

INTRUSIVE ROCKS can take **MILLIONS** of years to form.

Volcanoes

Magma usually reaches Earth's surface through volcanoes. First, the magma must rise toward Earth's surface. This happens when melting rock in Earth's interior releases gas. The gas mixes with magma and makes it lighter, causing it to rise.

Near the surface, magma collects in a chamber, or hollow area, under a volcano. As more and more magma enters the chamber, the space becomes full. This causes pressure to build. The magma eventually bursts through a channel to Earth's surface called a vent. The amount of gas in the magma affects the eruptions. The more gas there is, the more violent the eruption will be.

Volcanoes can look very different from one another. Their shape depends on what kinds of eruptions they have and how their lava flows and cools. Cone volcanoes have steep sides and a conelike shape. They are formed from the buildup of lava, ash, and rock over many eruptions. Shield volcanoes are low and broad. They are created when lava flows far from a volcano's vent before hardening.

1 A vent is created when the heat or pressure of built-up magma causes part of the wall of the magma chamber to melt or break.

2 A secondary vent is a smaller branch that forms off the main vent.

3 An eruption reduces the amount of magma in the chamber. Over time, new magma often enters the chamber. Then, the volcano may erupt again.

PARTS OF A VOLCANO

While there are many different kinds of volcanoes, most share certain features in common.

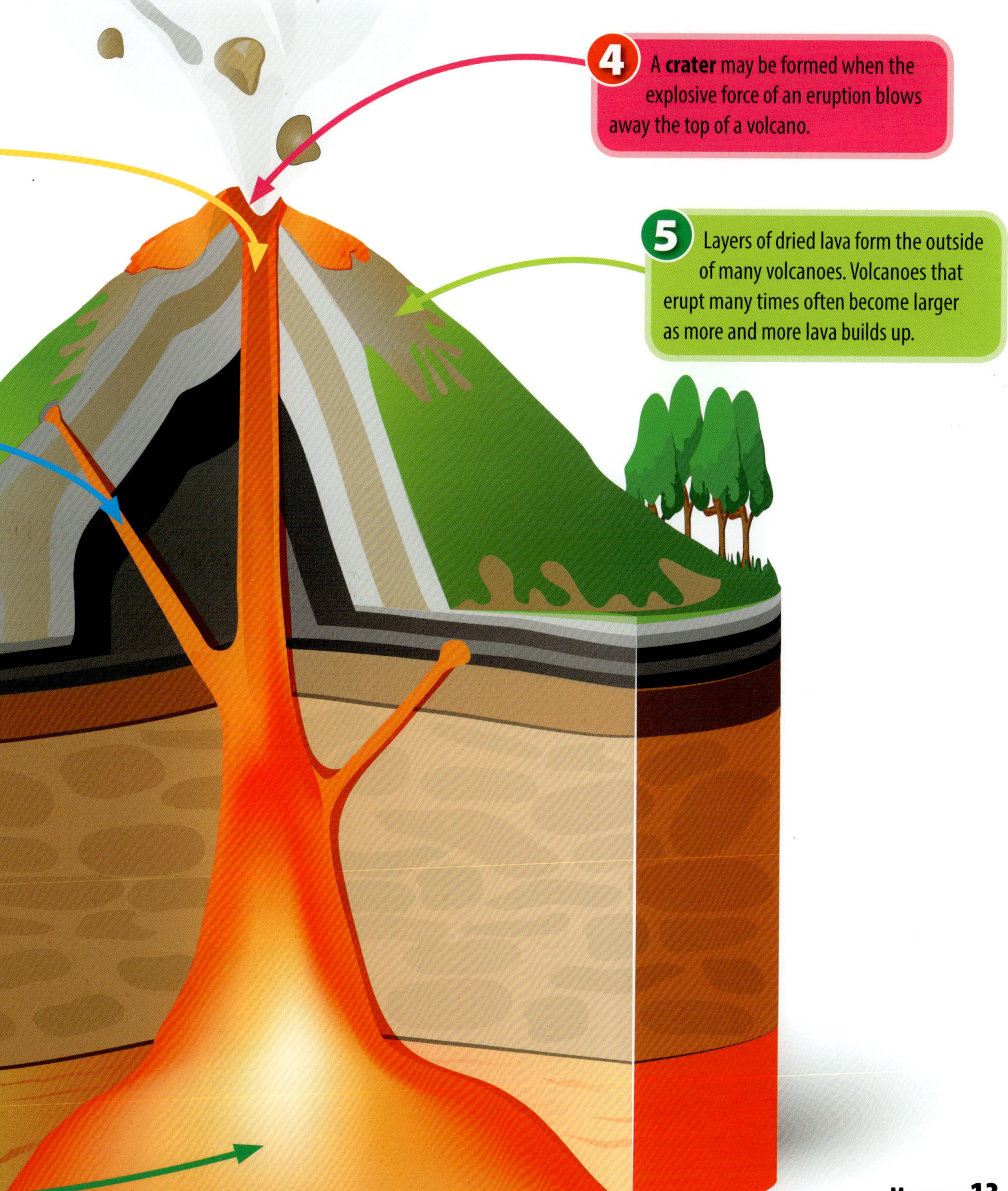

Volcanoes around the World

Earth's crust, along with the top part of its mantle, is made of large blocks called tectonic plates. These plates make up the **lithosphere**. Magma flows beneath the tectonic plates. In spots where gaps allow it to reach the surface, it can erupt from volcanoes. Volcanoes can be found all over the world.

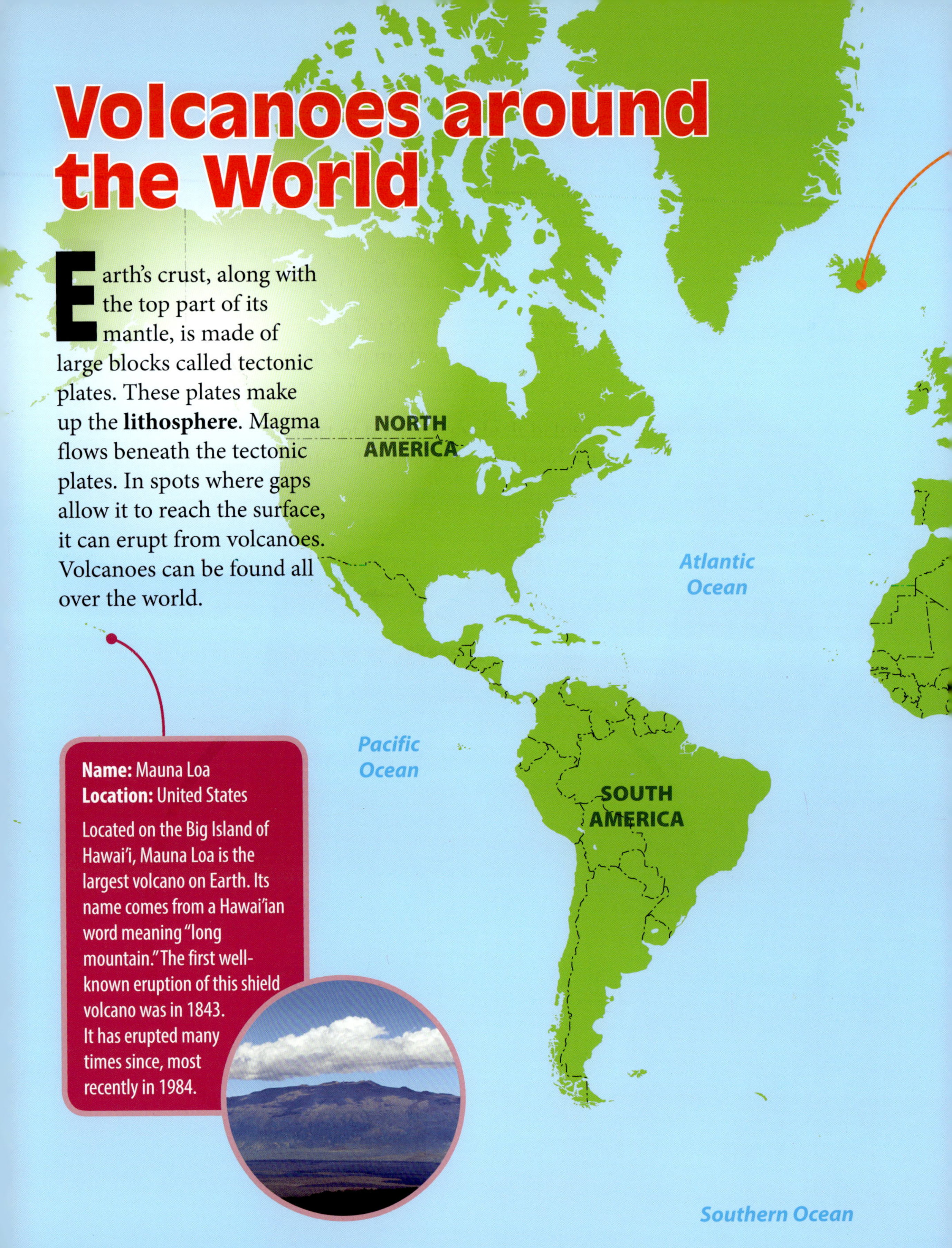

NORTH AMERICA

Atlantic Ocean

Pacific Ocean

SOUTH AMERICA

Name: Mauna Loa
Location: United States

Located on the Big Island of Hawai'i, Mauna Loa is the largest volcano on Earth. Its name comes from a Hawai'ian word meaning "long mountain." The first well-known eruption of this shield volcano was in 1843. It has erupted many times since, most recently in 1984.

Southern Ocean

Name: Eyjafjallajökull Volcano
Location: Iceland
Iceland is a country known for its volcanic activity. In 2010, a volcano underneath the Eyjafjalla Glacier erupted. Lava from the volcano caused large amounts of ice to melt, leading to floods. The volcano also created a cloud of steam and ash that rose more than 6.2 miles (10 kilometers). Many airlines in Europe had to cancel flights as a result.
Name: Mount Merapi
Location: Indonesia
Merapi is the most active volcano in Indonesia. Its name means "Mountain of Fire." Merapi rises 9,551 feet (2,911 meters) above sea level. Many of its eruptions have created pyroclastic flows. In 1994, an eruption caused more than 60 deaths.
EUROPE
ASIA
AFRICA
Indian Ocean
AUSTRALIA
Name: Mount Vesuvius
Location: Italy
Mount Vesuvius is more than 200,000 years old, making it a young volcano. Its best-known eruption was in 79 AD. The eruption covered the city of Pompeii, and other nearby towns, in ash and stone. The ruins of the city were covered in volcanic stone for more than 1,500 years.
Legend
Water
Land
N
W
E
S
Scale
0
2,000 Miles
2,000 Kilometers

Making Islands

Volcanoes can cause large amounts of damage to nearby settlements and endanger people around them. Lava flowing from an erupting volcano can destroy crops, roads, and buildings. However, lava can also be a force of creation. It is one of the methods by which new islands can be formed.

Islands created by underwater volcanoes are known as oceanic or volcanic islands. As volcanoes erupt underwater, they release lava, which quickly cools into solid igneous rock. Over time, layers of these rocks build up until they reach the surface of the water. A new island is created when this happens.

The magma that forms islands passes through Earth's crust in several ways. Some islands, such as those that make up Japan, form at places where one tectonic plate slides underneath another. The movement of these plates causes many volcanoes to form. Other volcanoes form when two plates move away from each other. Some islands, such as the Hawai'ian islands, are above a single tectonic plate.

Another term for oceanic islands is "high islands." Islands that broke away from another piece of land are sometimes called "low islands."

FORMING THE HAWAI'IAN ISLANDS

The Hawai'ian islands are located above a "hot spot." This is an area of Earth's mantle where magma is able to push upward through the crust. The hot spot stays in one place as the crust moves very slowly over it. The magma in Hawai'i's hot spot has created 82 different volcanoes. Over millions of years, this has led to the creation of the different islands that make up Hawai'i.

Today, Hawai'i's Big Island is the youngest Hawai'ian island. Located above the hot spot, it is home to the world's most active volcano, Kilauea. The Big Island is still volcanically active, making it the largest in size. Older islands, such as Kauai to the west, have been worn down by ocean waves. In tens of thousands of years, a new island may form when a volcano known as the Lō'ihi Seamount rises above the ocean to the east of the Big Island.

The state of Hawai'i includes 8 major islands and more than 120 smaller islands.

Magma Timeline

Magma has impacted history in many ways. As scientists become more able to study magma, they are better able to understand how Earth was formed. They are also better able to help when dangerous eruptions occur.

The last eruption of Mauna Kea in Hawai'i takes place. Like other volcanoes in Hawai'i, it mainly produces basalt.

4000 years ago

1862

1963

Lord Kelvin, a Scottish physicist, estimates Earth's age by measuring how quickly **molten** rocks cool.

An underwater volcanic eruption takes place off the coast of Iceland. As the lava cools, it leads to the creation of a new island. It is named Surtsey after Surtur, an Icelandic fire god.

Drillers in Hawai'i accidentally drill into a pocket of magma. This allows people to study magma underground for the first time.

The Hawai'ian volcano Kilauea begins erupting in May. Lava covers 13.7 square miles (35.5 square kilometers) of land and destroys more than 700 homes. However, lava reaching the ocean and cooling also creates 875 acres (354 hectares) of new land.

2008 **2015** **2018**

Researchers from the University of Utah discover a massive magma chamber beneath Yellowstone National Park. It holds enough magma to fill 11 Grand Canyons.

Quiz

Now that you have read all about lava and magma, test your knowledge by answering these questions. All of the information can be found in the text you just read. The answers are provided below for easy reference.

1 What is the hottest kind of magma?

4 What kinds of rocks come from lava?

7 What is a "hot spot"?

10 What kind of magma forms block lava?

ANSWER KEY

1 Basaltic magma
2 Surtur, an Icelandic fire god
3 Indonesia
4 Igneous rocks
5 Through volcanoes
6 Pahoehoe
7 An area of Earth's mantle where magma is able to push upward through the crust
8 A smaller branch that forms off the main vent
9 No
10 Andesitic or rhyolitic magma

2 What is the island of Surtsey named after?

3 Where is Mount Merapi located?

6 Which type of lava flows by extending "toes" of lava?

5 How does magma reach Earth's surface?

8 What is a volcano's secondary vent?

9 Is Earth's crust completely solid?

Make a Volcano

Follow these instructions to create your own volcano. This activity should be done with an adult.

BEFORE YOU START, YOU WILL NEED

1. Put the soda bottle into the baking pan. Mold the modeling clay around the bottle in the shape of a volcano. Make sure no clay goes into the bottle.
2. Let the clay dry for two days.
3. Use the funnel to fill the bottle most of the way with warm water. Add food coloring to the water until it changes color.
4. Add the liquid dishwashing soap.
5. Add the baking soda and vinegar to the bottle.
6. Watch for the eruption. If liquid does not bubble up fast enough, add a little more vinegar.
7. Once your volcano has finished erupting, look at where your "lava" traveled. How much of the volcano did it cover? What does this tell you about how lava would change the shape of a volcano as it dries?

Key Words

active: at risk of erupting

crater: a bowl-shaped area at the top of a volcano created by past eruptions

crust: Earth's hard, outer layer

erosion: the removal of rock and pieces of soil by natural forces such as running water, ice, waves, and wind

erupts: sends out material with great force

lithosphere: the outer shell of Earth, made up of the crust and upper mantle

mantle: the mostly-solid layer of Earth below the planet's crust and above its core

minerals: natural substances that are not animals or plants

molten: objects that are so hot they become liquid

pyroclastic flows: walls of hot rocks and gas that move quickly down the side of a volcano

recycle: to reuse materials

rock cycle: the process by which rocks change from one type of rock to another over time

sediments: sand and dirt that settle to the bottom of a river or lake

sills: layers of igneous rock that form between layers of other kinds of rock, such as sedimentary rock

volcanoes: mountains or hills with openings that provide a path for magma from Earth's core to reach the surface

weathering: when rocks are broken down into smaller pieces by rain, ice, or wind without being moved

Index

LIGHTBOX

SUPPLEMENTARY RESOURCES

Click on the plus icon found in the bottom left corner of each spread to open additional teacher resources.

- Download and print the book's quizzes and activities
- Access curriculum correlations
- Explore additional web applications that enhance the Lightbox experience

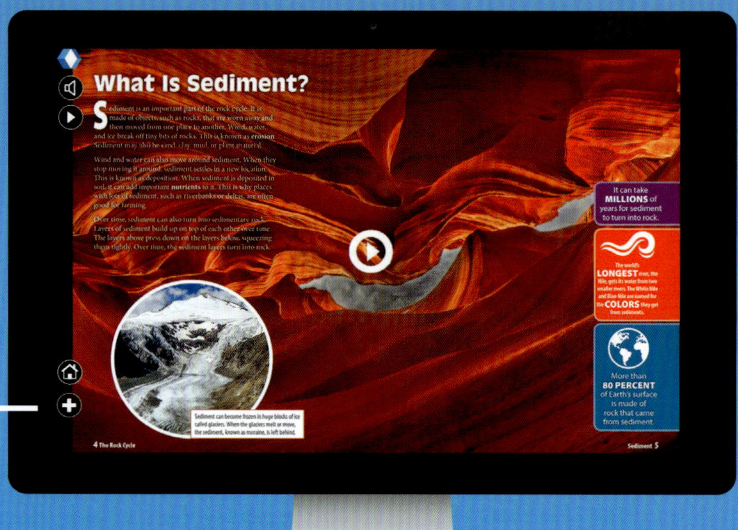

LIGHTBOX DIGITAL TITLES

Packed full of integrated media

VIDEOS

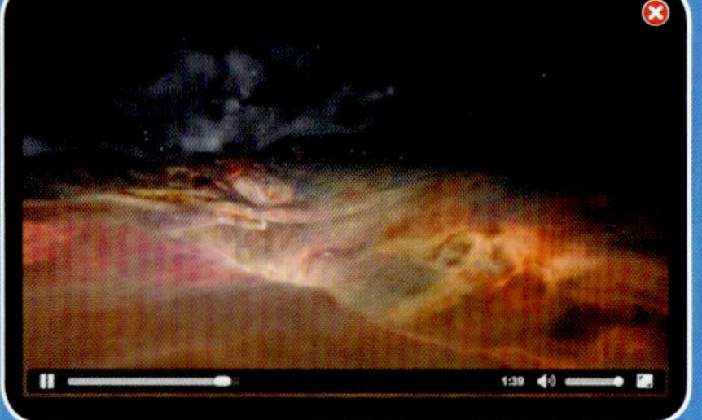

INTERACTIVE MAPS

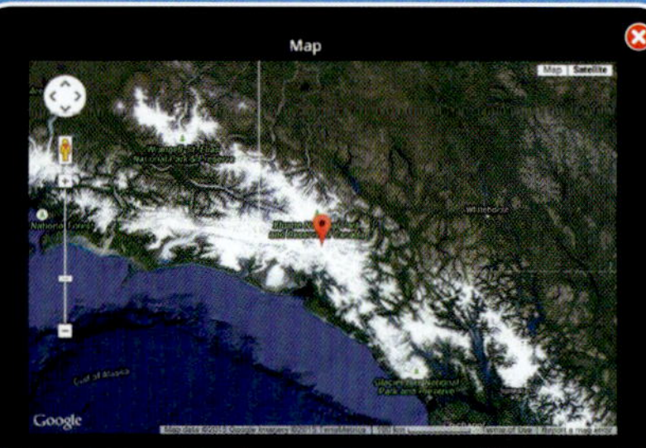

WEBLINKS

SLIDESHOWS

QUIZZES

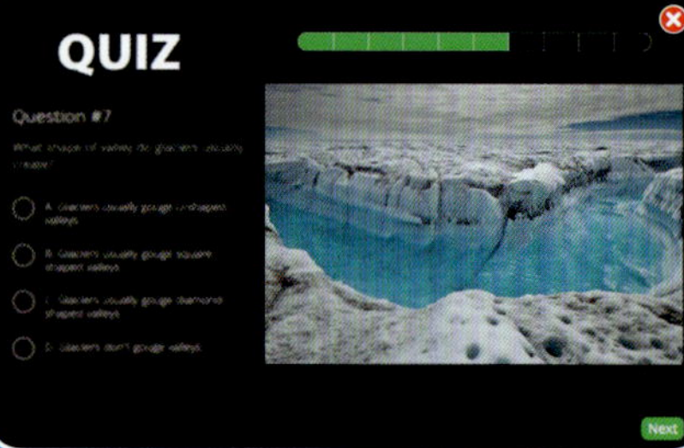

OPTIMIZED FOR

- ✔ TABLETS
- ✔ WHITEBOARDS
- ✔ COMPUTERS
- ✔ AND MUCH MORE!

Published by Smartbook Media Inc.
350 5th Avenue, 59th Floor New York, NY 10118
Website: www.openlightbox.com

Library of Congress Control Number: 2019942191

ISBN 978-1-5105-4440-6 (hardcover)
ISBN 978-1-5105-4441-3 (multi-user eBook)

Printed in Guangzhou, China
1 2 3 4 5 6 7 8 9 0 23 22 21 20 19

072019
122818

Project Coordinator John Willis
Graphic Designer Ana María Vidal

Photo Credits
Every reasonable effort has been made to trace ownership and to obtain permission to reprint copyright material. The publisher would be pleased to have any errors or omissions brought to its attention so that it may be corrected in subsequent printings. The publisher acknowledges Alamy, Dreamstime, Getty Images, iStock, Newscom, and Shutterstock as its primary image suppliers for this title.